Name Danny

Date

1 Apple

■ Trace each step while looking at the sample drawing.
   Remember to add color to your object in the last step!

Sample

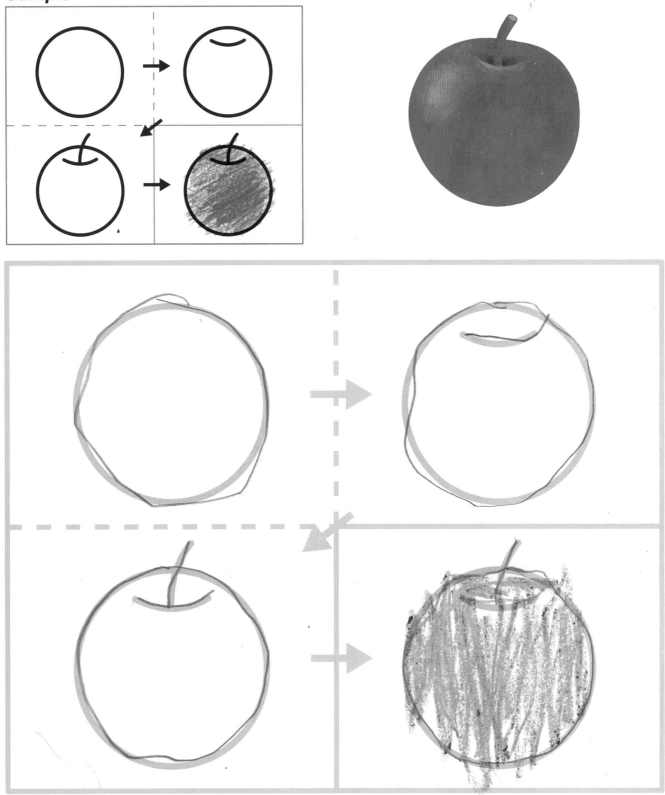

■ Now try drawing some apples of your own!

2 Baseball

Name

Date

■ Trace each step while looking at the sample drawing.
Remember to add color to your object in the last step!

Sample

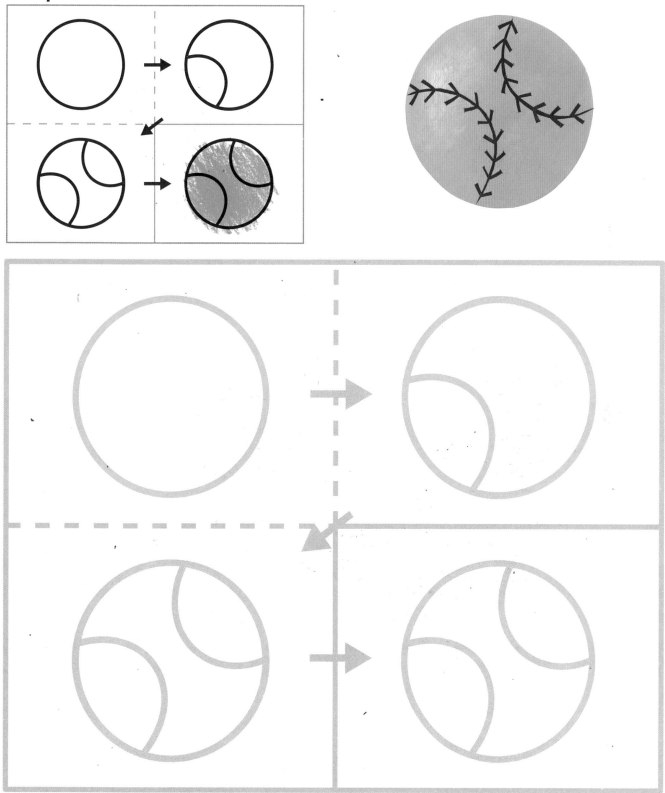

3

■ Now try drawing some baseballs of your own!

3 Balloon

Name

Date

■ Trace each step while looking at the sample drawing.
Remember to add color to your object in the last step!

Sample

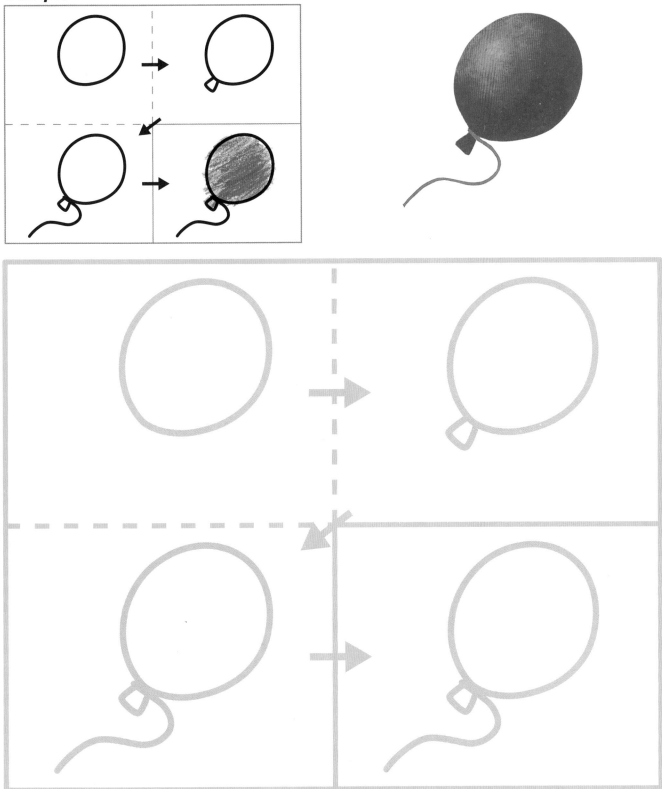

■ Now try drawing some balloons of your own!

Orange

Name

Date

■ Trace each step while looking at the sample drawing.
Remember to add color to your object in the last step!

Sample

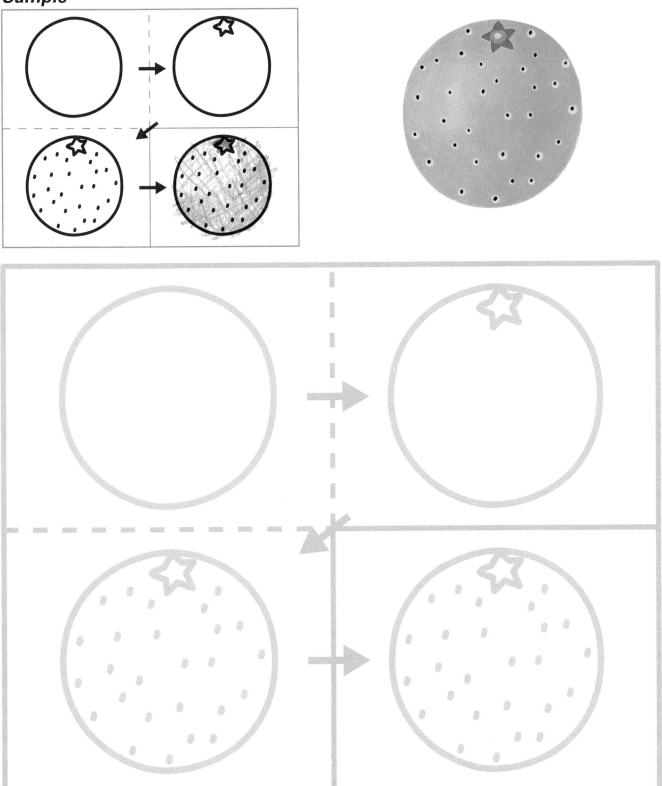

7

■ Now try drawing some oranges of your own!

Cherries

■ Trace each step while looking at the sample drawing.
Remember to add color to your object in the last step!

Sample

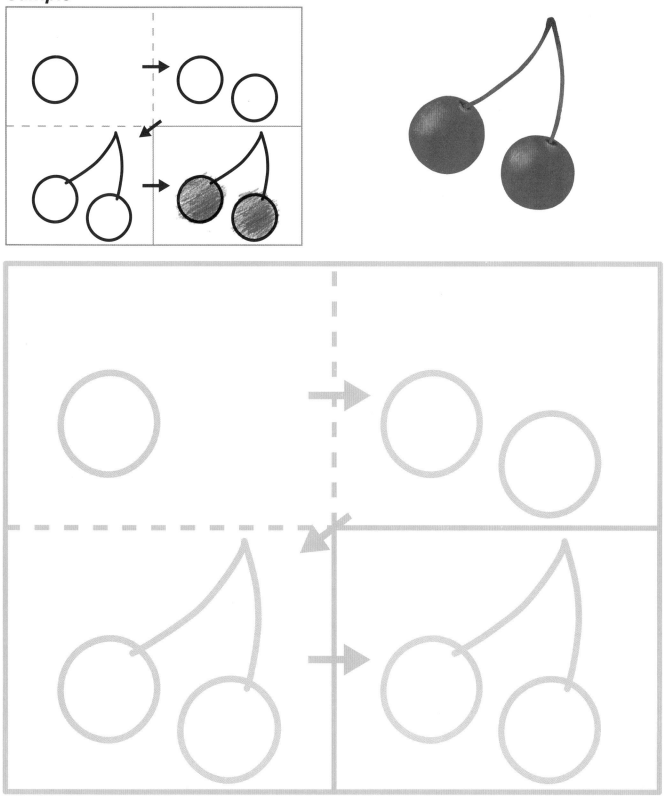

■ Now try drawing some cherries of your own!

6 Fried Egg

Name
Date

■ Trace each step while looking at the sample drawing.
  Remember to add color to your object in the last step!

Sample

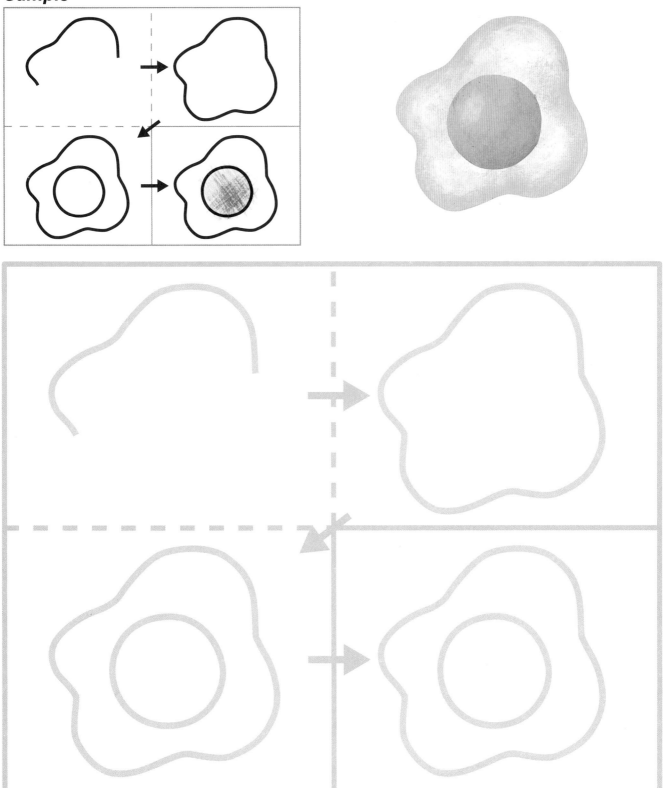

■ Now try drawing some fried eggs of your own!

Snow Cone

Name
Date

■ Trace each step while looking at the sample drawing.
  Remember to add color to your object in the last step!

Sample

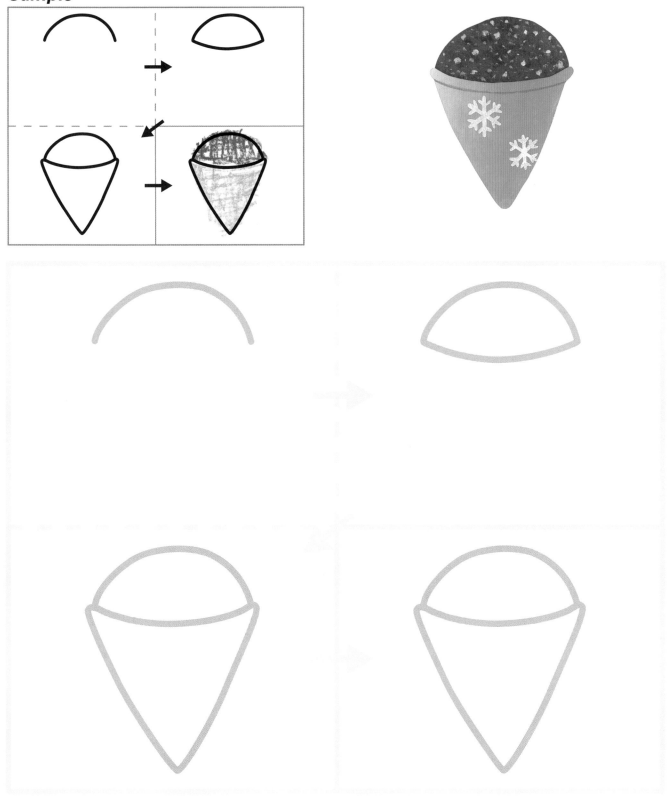

■ Now try drawing some snow cones of your own!

8 Acorn

Name

Date

■ Trace each step while looking at the sample drawing. Remember to add color to your object in the last step!

Sample

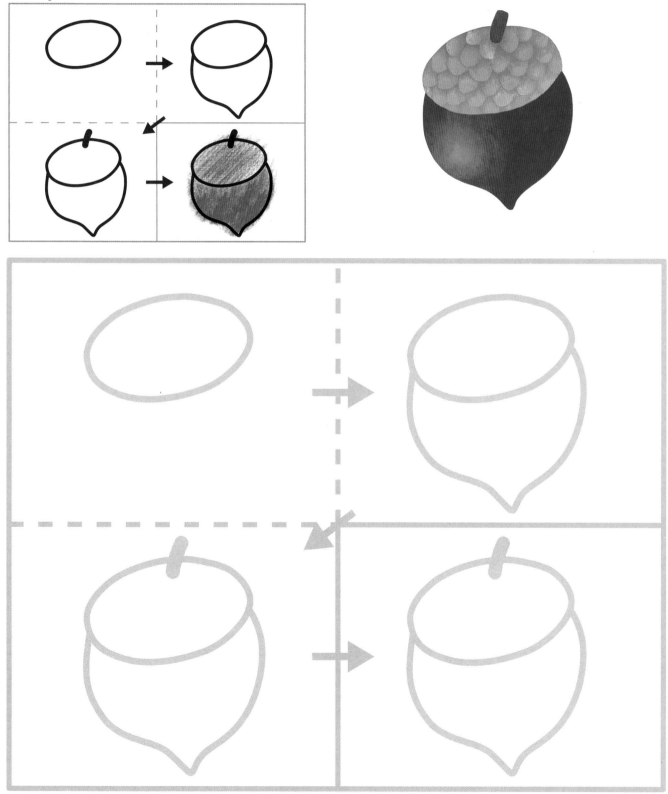

15

■ Now try drawing some acorns of your own!

■ Trace each step while looking at the sample drawing.
Remember to add color to your object in the last step!

Sample

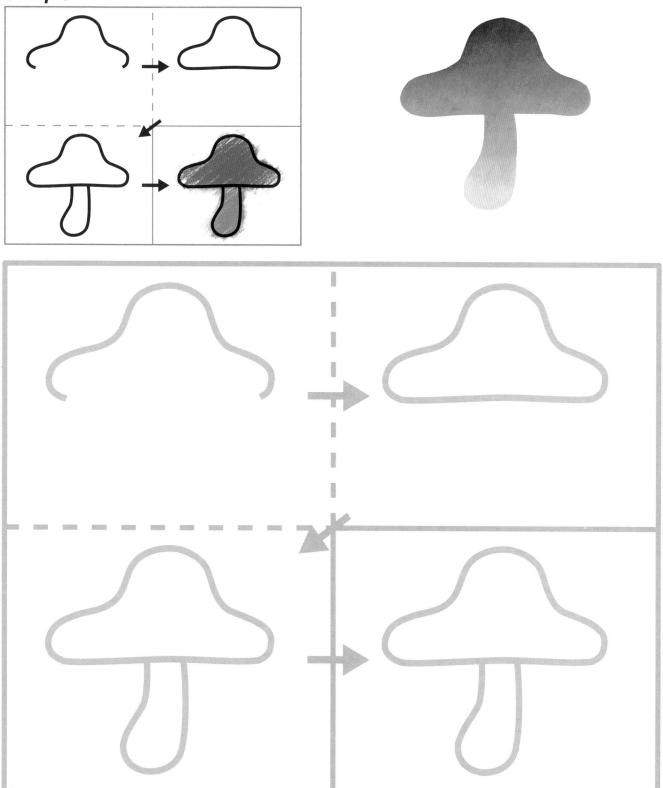

■ Now try drawing some mushrooms of your own!

Eggplant

■ Trace each step while looking at the sample drawing.
Remember to add color to your object in the last step!

Sample

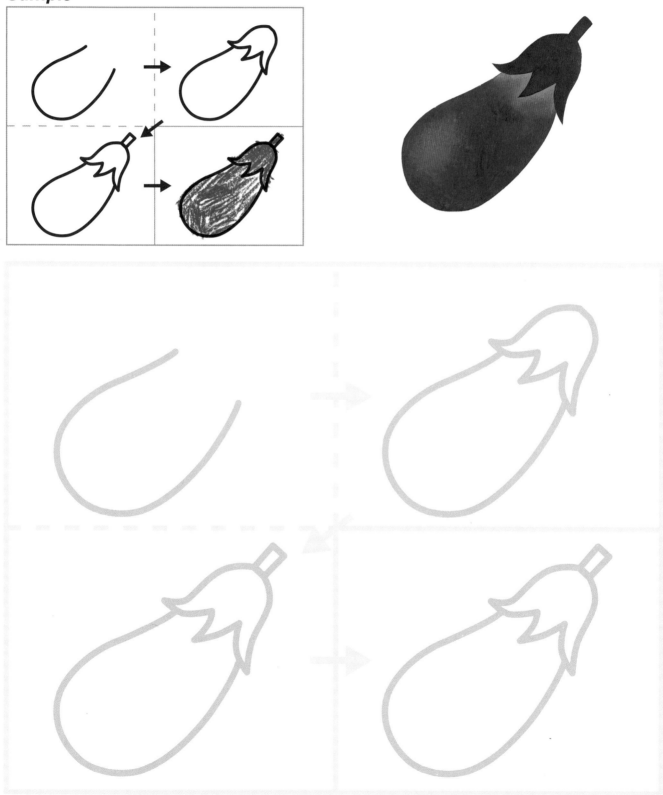

■ Now try drawing some eggplants of your own!

Hot Dog

Name

Date

■ Trace each step while looking at the sample drawing.
Remember to add color to your object in the last step!

Sample

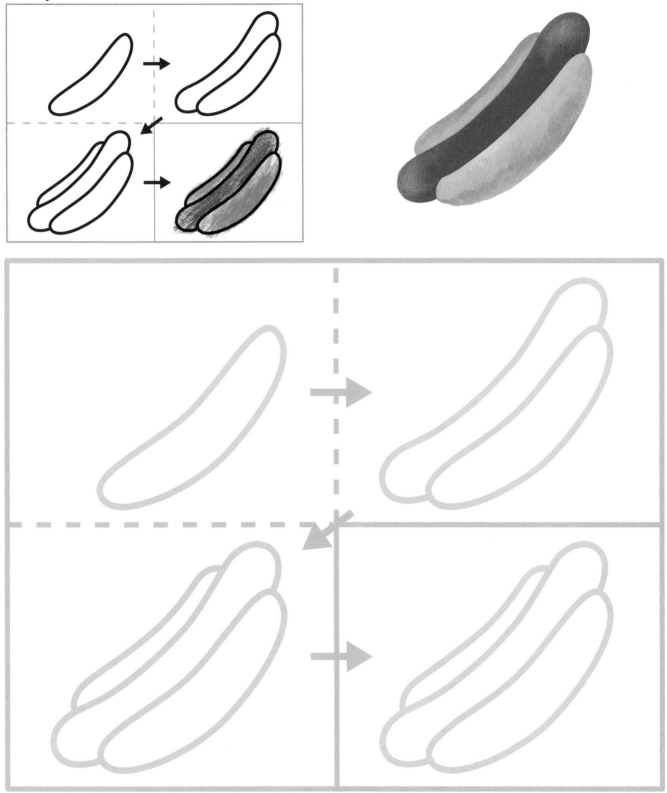

■ Now try drawing some hot dogs of your own!

Strawberry

■ Trace each step while looking at the sample drawing.
Remember to add color to your object in the last step!

Sample

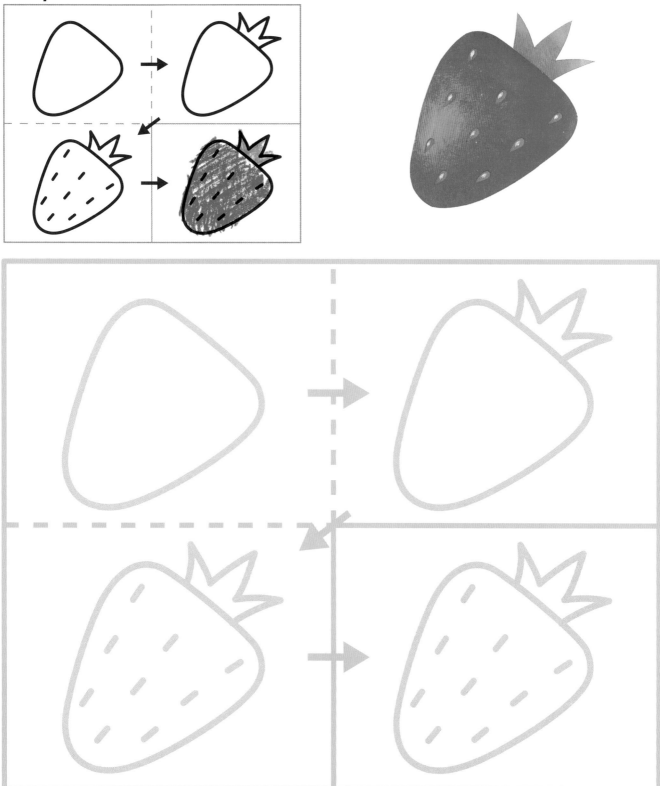

■ Now try drawing some strawberries of your own!

Hamburger

Name

Date

■ Trace each step while looking at the sample drawing.
Remember to add color to your object in the last step!

Sample

■ Now try drawing some hamburgers of your own!

 **Boot**

Name

Date

■ Trace each step while looking at the sample drawing.
Remember to add color to your object in the last step!

Sample

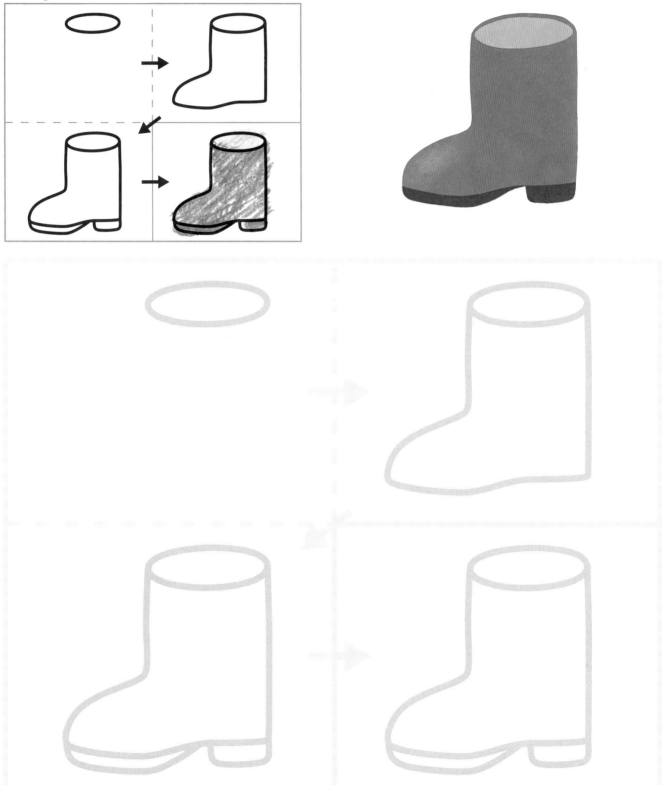

27

■ Now try drawing some boots of your own!

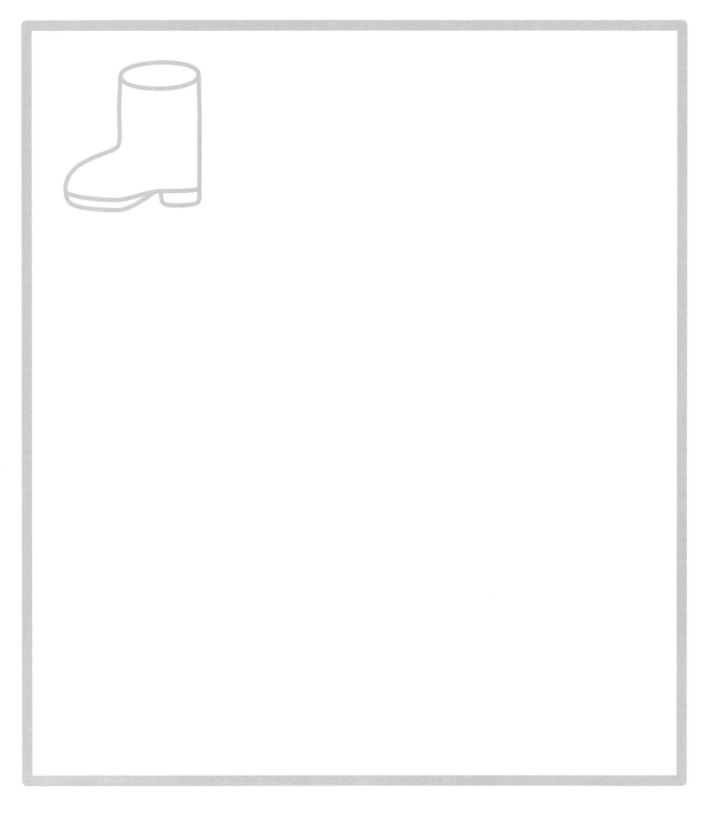

Cap

Name

Date

■ Trace each step while looking at the sample drawing.
Remember to add color to your object in the last step!

Sample

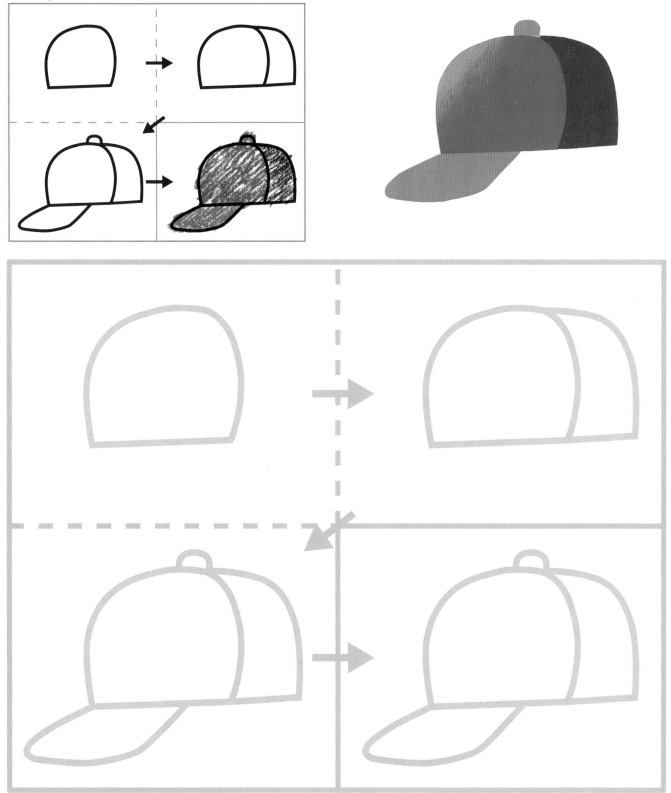

■ Now try drawing some caps of your own!

16 Watermelon

Name	
Date	

■ Trace each step while looking at the sample drawing.
Remember to add color to your object in the last step!

Sample

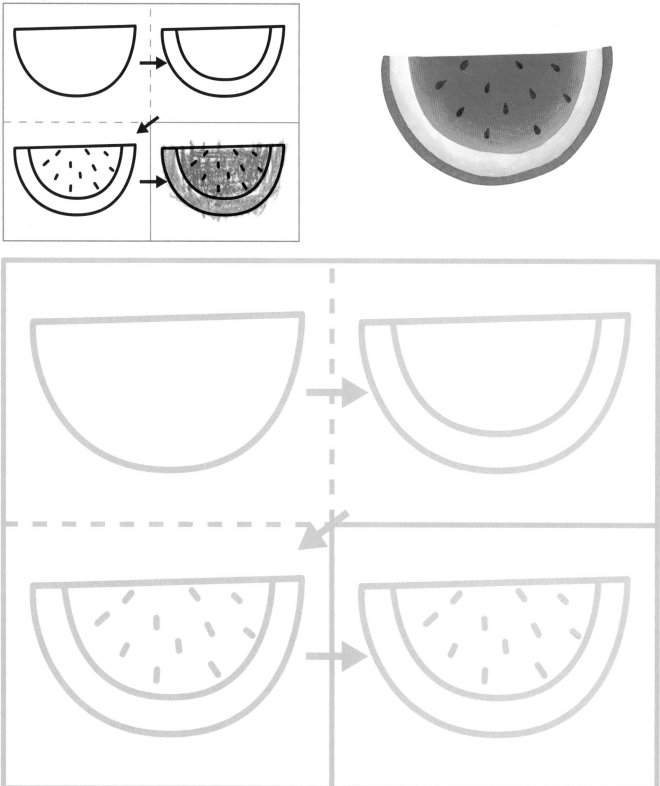

■ Now try drawing some watermelons of your own!

17 **Shirt**

■ Trace each step while looking at the sample drawing.
Remember to add color to your object in the last step!

Sample

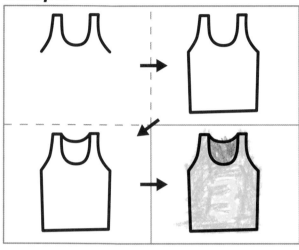

33

■ Now try drawing some shirts of your own!

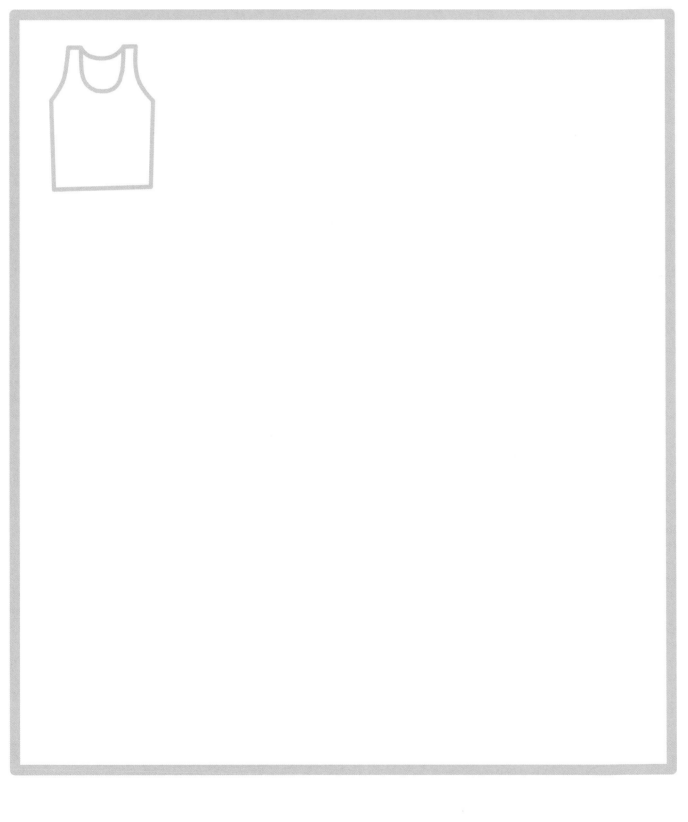

Name

Date

■ Trace each step while looking at the sample drawing.
Remember to add color to your object in the last step!

Sample

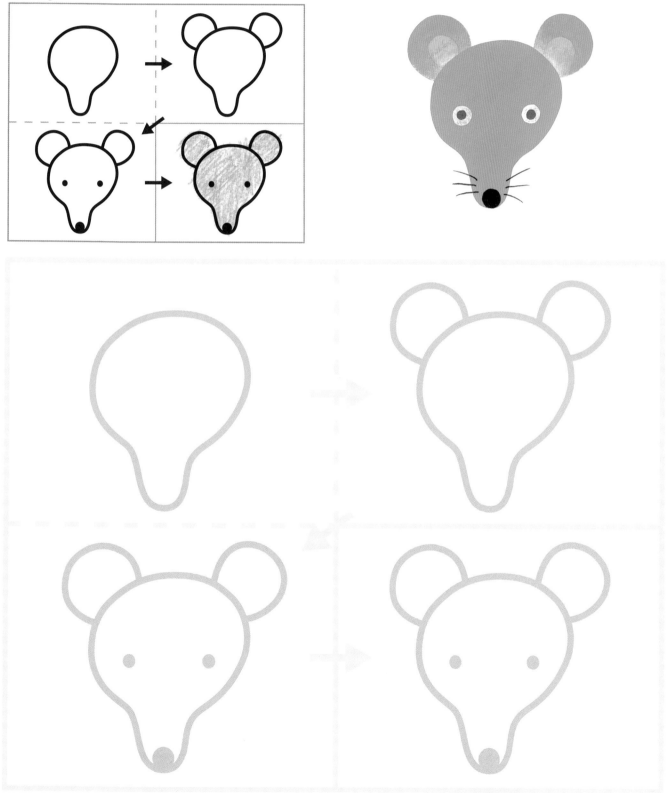

■ Now try drawing some mice of your own!

Bear

■ Trace each step while looking at the sample drawing.
  Remember to add color to your object in the last step!

Sample

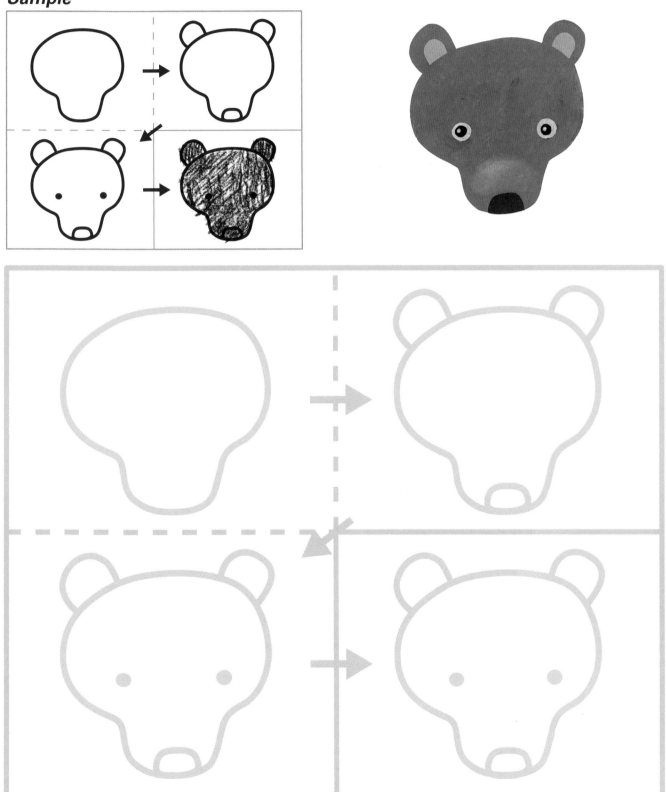

■ Now try drawing some bears of your own!

20 Dog

■ Trace each step while looking at the sample drawing.
Remember to add color to your object in the last step!

Sample

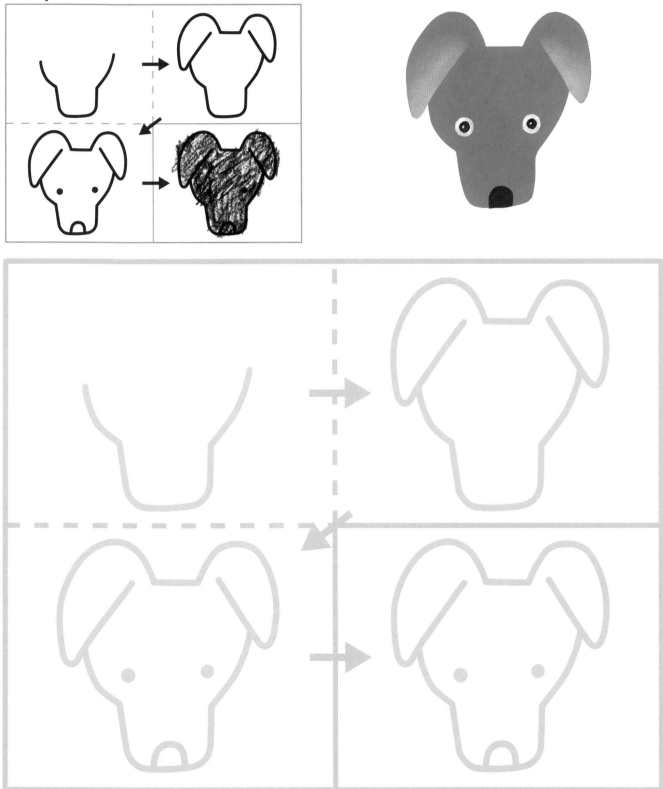

■ Now try drawing some dogs of your own!

 **Fox**

■ Trace each step while looking at the sample drawing.
  Remember to add color to your object in the last step!

Sample

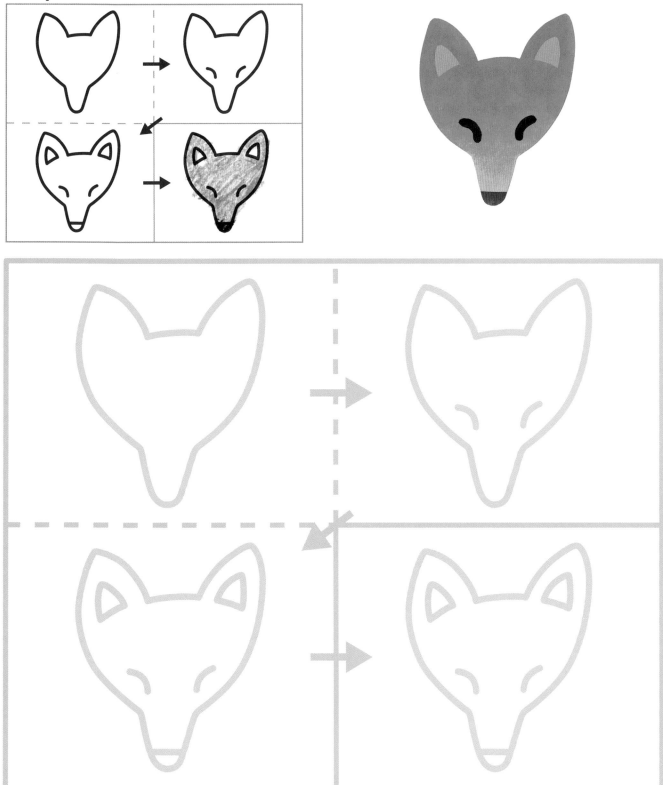

■ Now try drawing some foxes of your own!

22 **Cupcake**

■ Trace each step while looking at the sample drawing.
Remember to add color to your object in the last step!

Sample

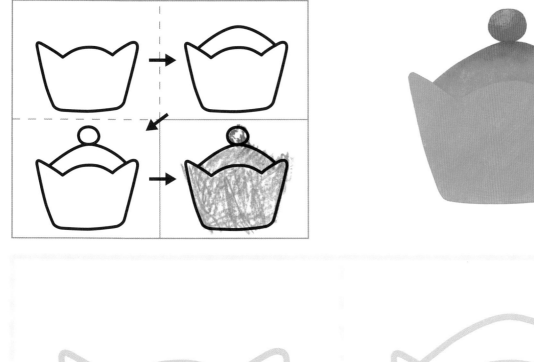

■ Now try drawing some cupcakes of your own!

Tulip

■ Trace each step while looking at the sample drawing.
Remember to add color to your object in the last step!

Sample

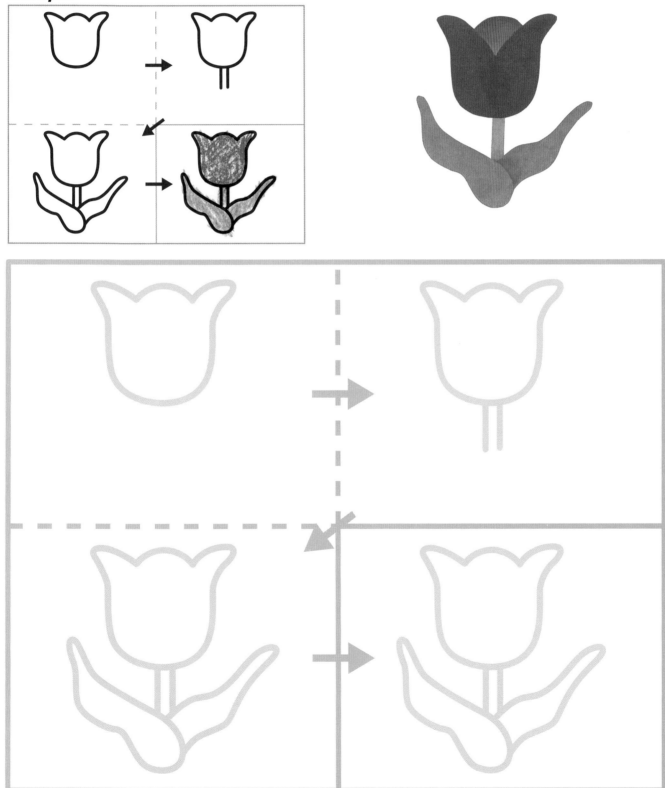

■ Now try drawing some tulips of your own!

 **24** **Spoon**

Name

Date

■ Trace each step while looking at the sample drawing.
Remember to add color to your object in the last step!

Sample

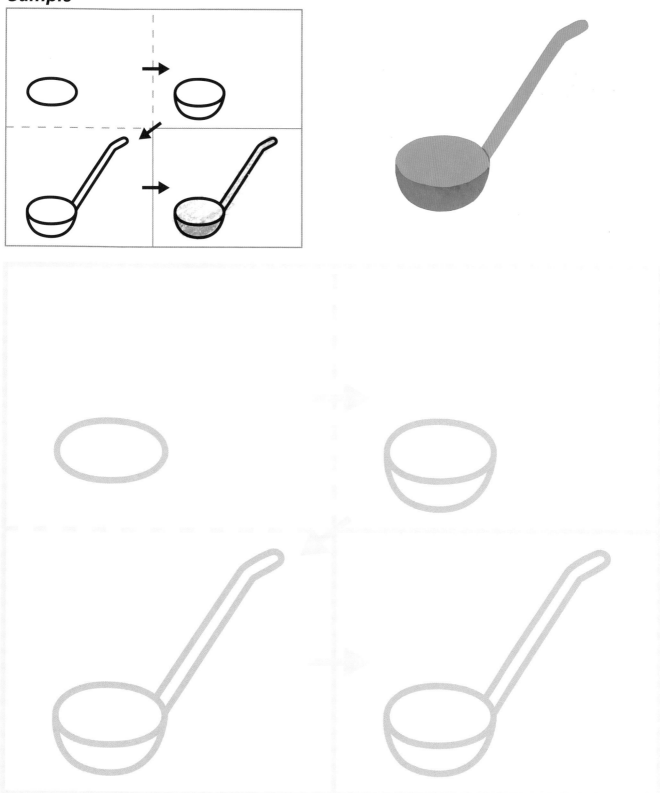

■ Now try drawing some spoons of your own!

Pan

Name	
Date	

■ Trace each step while looking at the sample drawing.
Remember to add color to your object in the last step!

Sample

Now try drawing some pans of your own!

 **Whale**

Name

Date

■ Trace each step while looking at the sample drawing.
Remember to add color to your object in the last step!

Sample

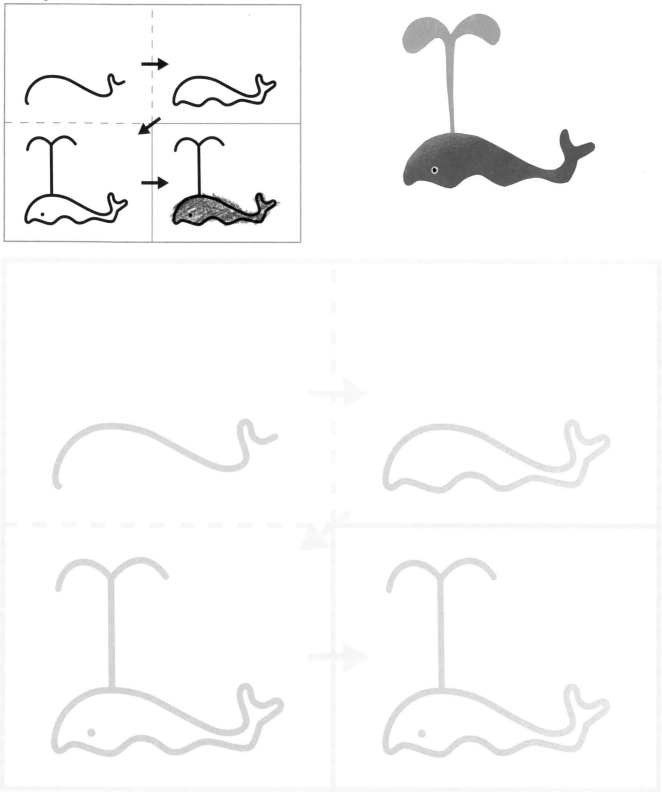

■ Now try drawing some whales of your own!

Kite

Name

Date

■ Trace each step while looking at the sample drawing. Remember to add color to your object in the last step!

Sample

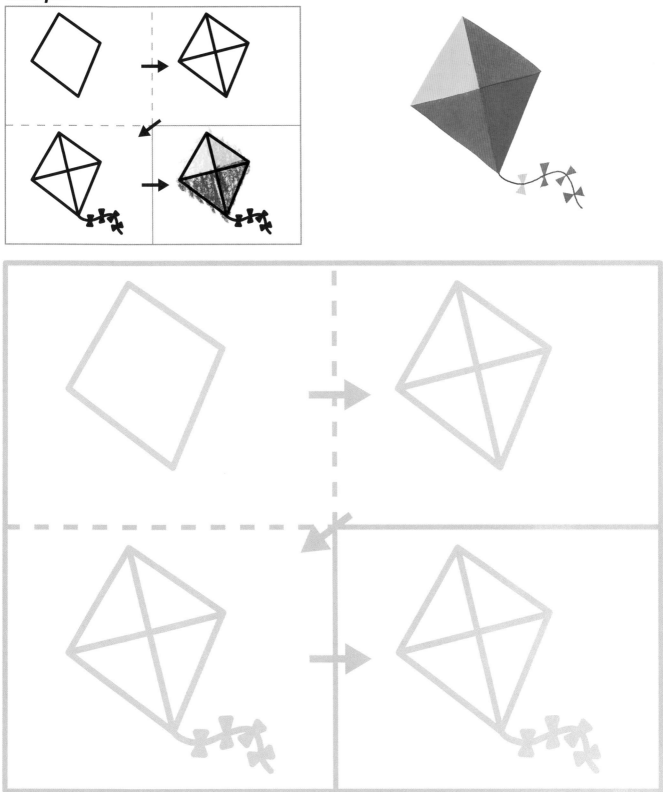

■ Now try drawing some kites of your own!

Mug

■ Trace each step while looking at the sample drawing.
  Remember to add color to your object in the last step!

Sample

■ Now try drawing some mugs of your own!

29 **Lunchbox**

■ Trace each step while looking at the sample drawing.
Remember to add color to your object in the last step!

Sample

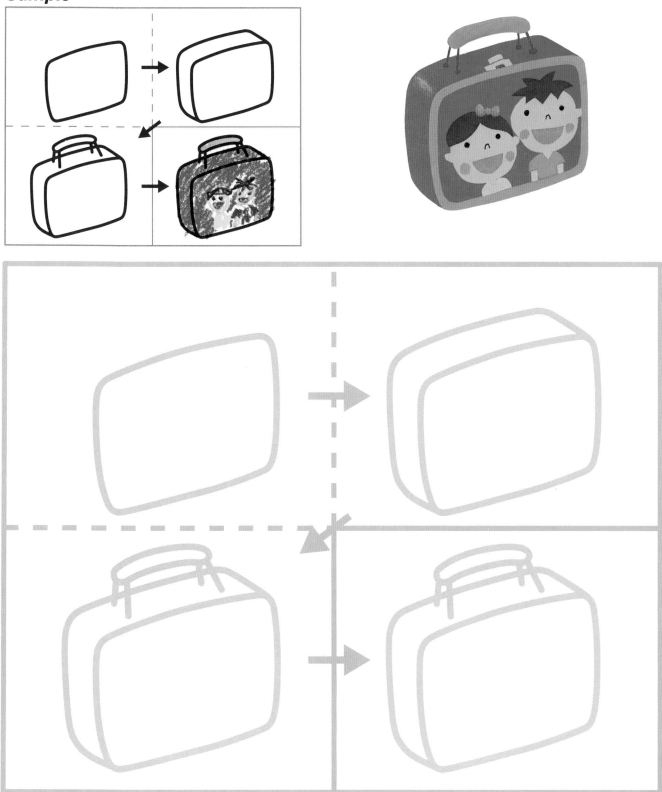

■ Now try drawing some lunchboxes of your own!

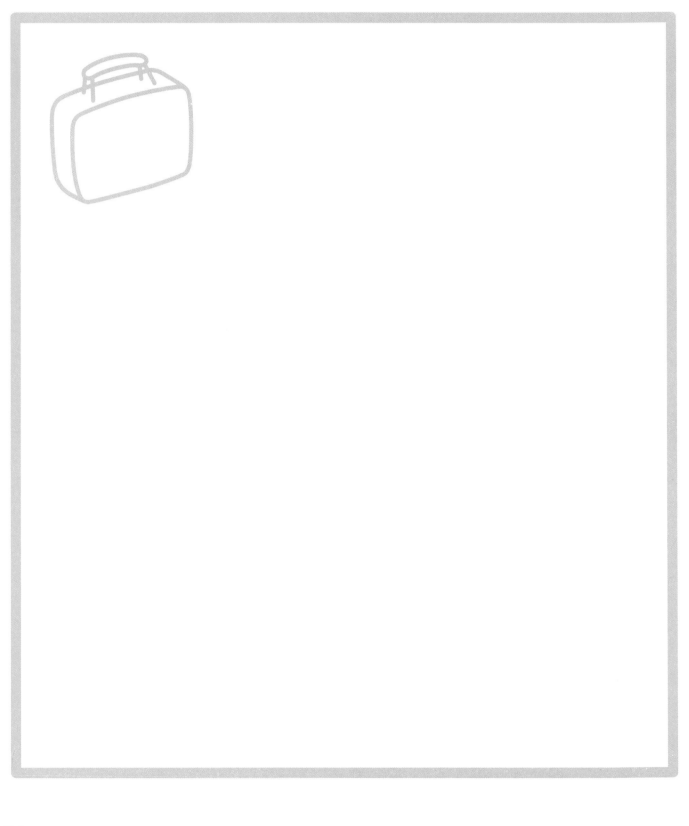

Baby Bottle

Name

Date

■ Trace each step while looking at the sample drawing.
Remember to add color to your object in the last step!

Sample

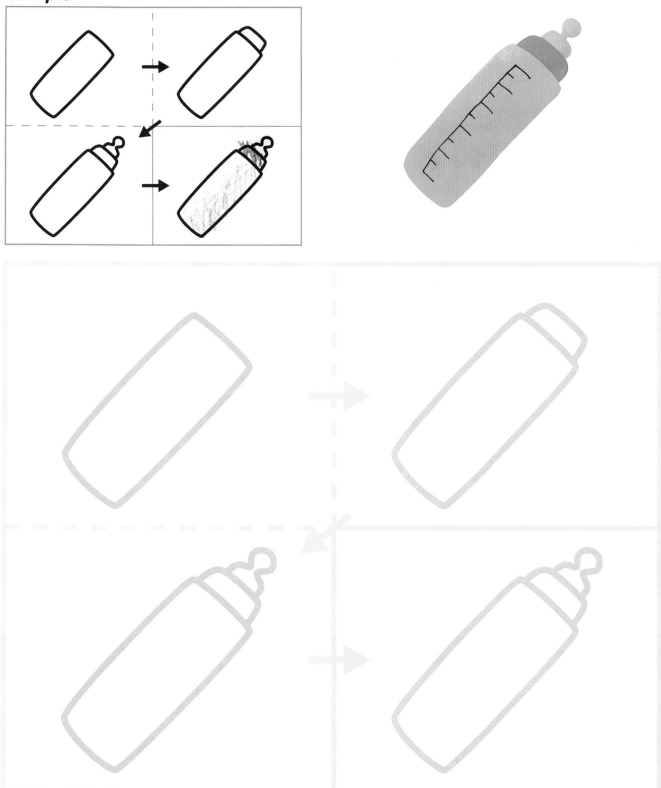

■ Now try drawing some baby bottles of your own!

 **31** **Key**

■ Trace each step while looking at the sample drawing.
Remember to add color to your object in the last step!

Sample

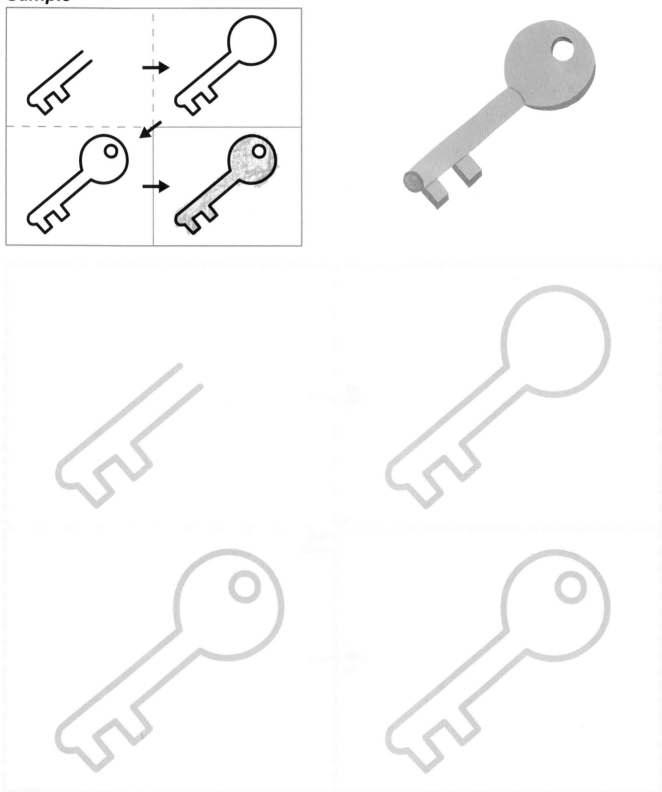

■ Now try drawing some keys of your own!

 **Bat**

Name

Date

■ Trace each step while looking at the sample drawing.
Remember to add color to your object in the last step!

Sample

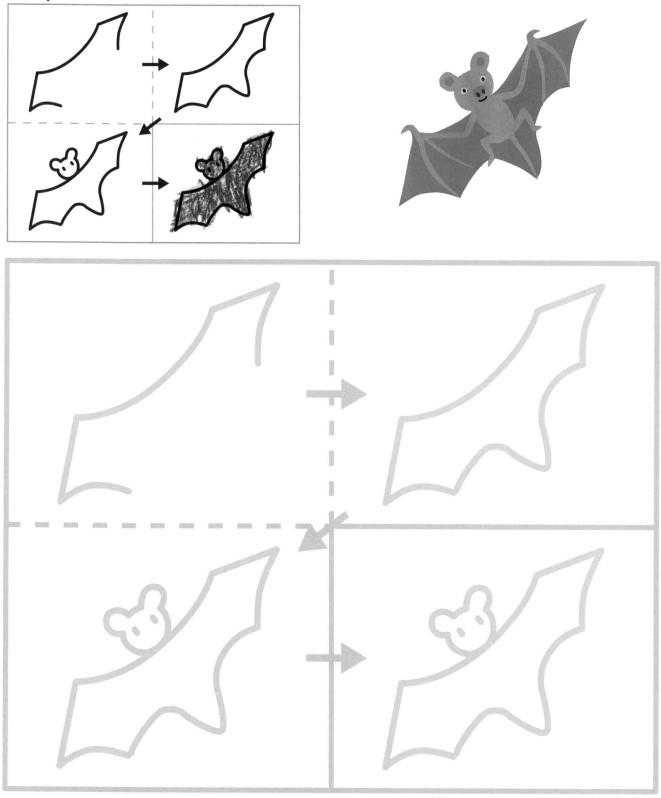

■ Now try drawing some bats of your own!

Name

Date

■ Trace each step while looking at the sample drawing.
Remember to add color to your object in the last step!

Sample

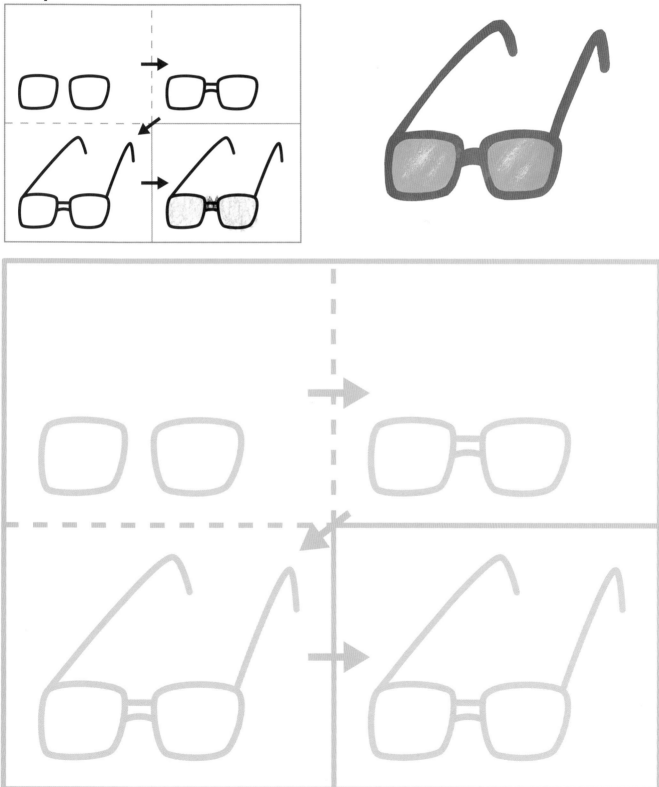

■ Now try drawing some glasses of your own!

Parachute

Name
Date

■ Trace each step while looking at the sample drawing.
Remember to add color to your object in the last step!

Sample

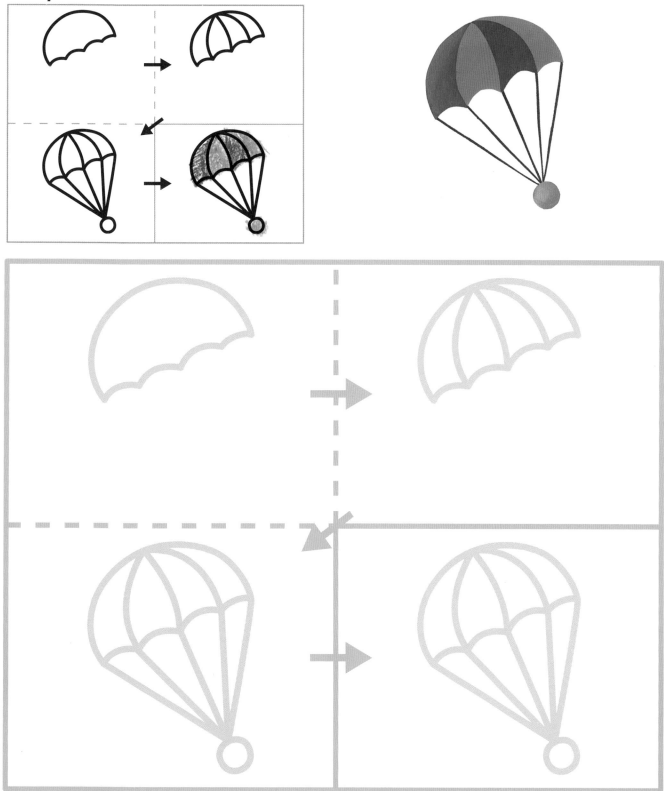

■ Now try drawing some parachutes of your own!

Name
Date

■ Trace each step while looking at the sample drawing.
Remember to add color to your object in the last step!

Sample

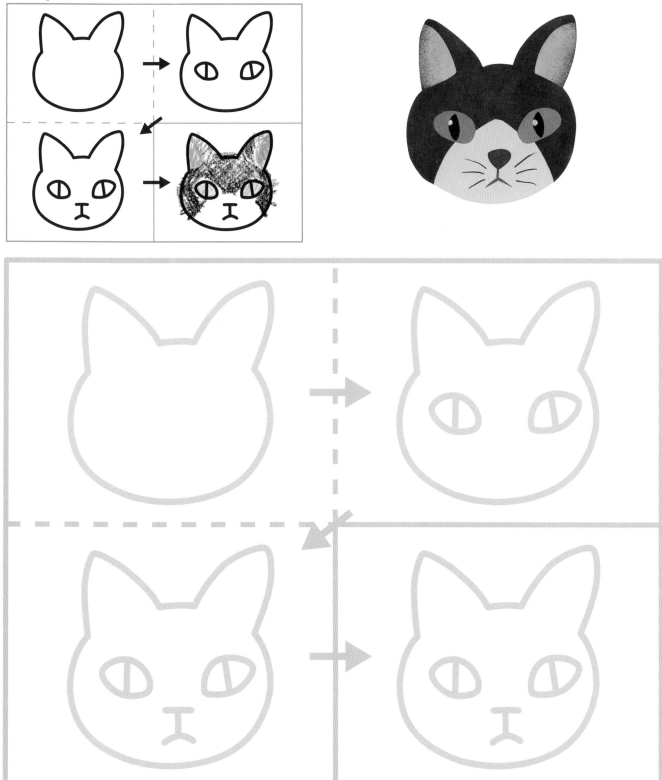

■ Now try drawing some cats of your own!

Clown Face

Name

Date

■ Trace each step while looking at the sample drawing.
   Remember to add color to your object in the last step!

Sample

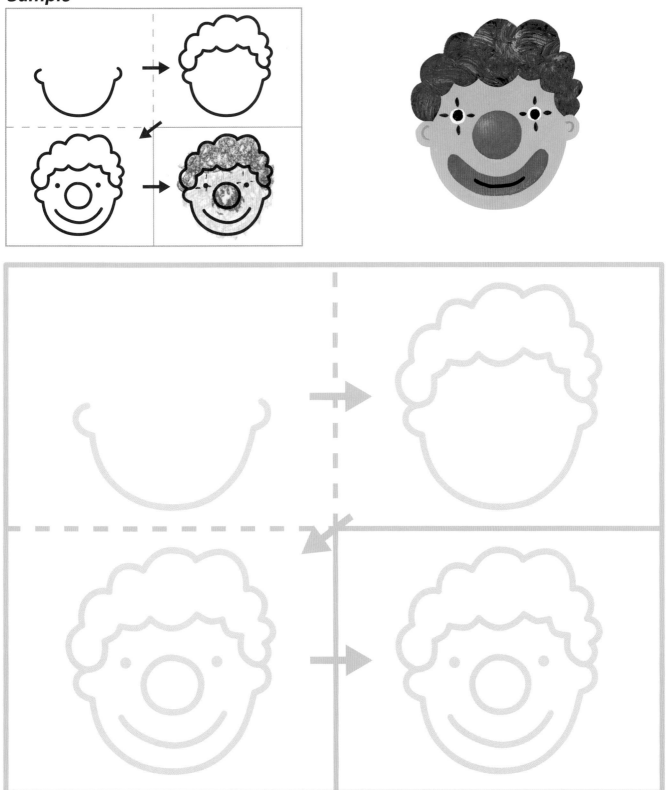

■ Now try drawing some clown faces of your own!

 **Die**

Name

Date

■ Trace each step while looking at the sample drawing. Remember to add color to your object in the last step!

Sample

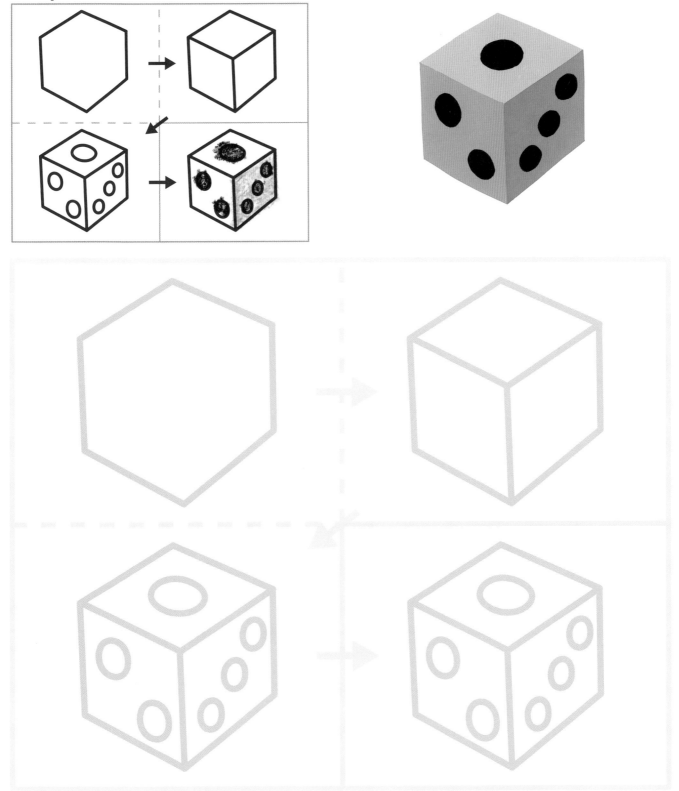

■ Now try drawing some dice of your own!

 **Blocks**

Name
Date

■ Trace each step while looking at the sample drawing.
 Remember to add color to your object in the last step!

Sample

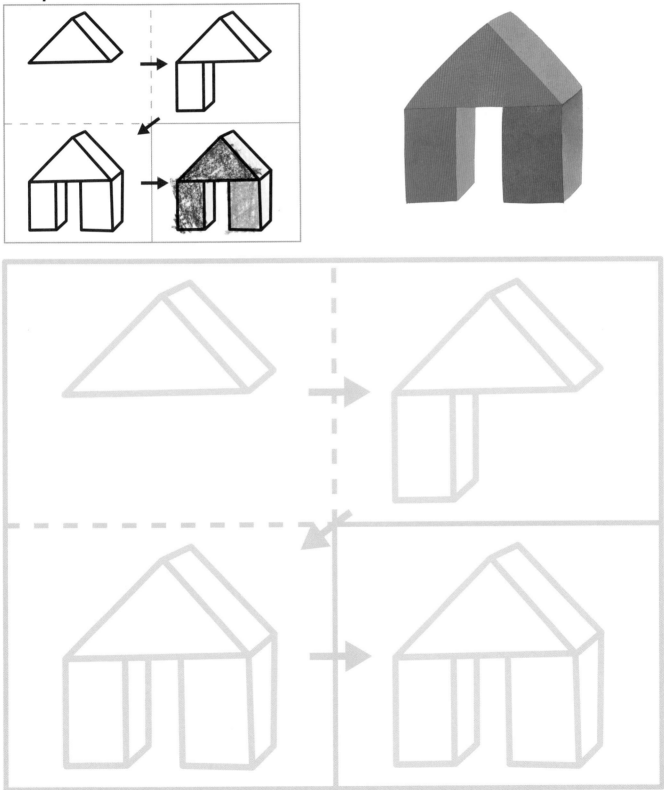

75

■ Now try drawing some blocks of your own!

Kettle

Name

Date

■ Trace each step while looking at the sample drawing.
Remember to add color to your object in the last step!

Sample

■ Now try drawing some kettles of your own!

 **Doll**

■ Trace each step while looking at the sample drawing.
Remember to add color to your object in the last step!

Sample

■ Now try drawing some dolls of your own!

Certificate of Achievement

_____

is hereby congratulated on completing

My First Book of Drawing

Presented on _____ , 20 ____

_____
Parent or Guardian